Trauma II Triumph

Memoir of Ronnie Lynn

Ronnie Lynn Sledge

Dedication

My memoir is dedicated to every person who has suffered emotional, physical and/or sexual trauma. To every person who suffered through being bullied and suffered negative outcomes such as substance abuse and mental health challenges. To those who have endured suicidal thoughts from the weight of the world on your shoulders. Finally, to those who are searching for love, acceptance, and healing. My prayer is that you would learn to love yourself, accept yourself with flaws and all, then actively work on your healing. Don’t get stuck in the past. Own who you are and work every day to become something greater.

Acknowledgment

First of all, God, thank you for never taking your hands off of me and for wrapping your loving arms around me, keeping my mind when I should have lost it, and putting the pieces of my heart back together over and over again when it was shattered by humanity, and for protecting me from dangers seen and unseen, and for guiding me to who you wanted me to be, I could not say thank you enough.

To my husband, Adrian: You are the best thing that ever happened to me outside God. Because of you, I am who I am today. Your constant love, support, and encouragement have not gone unnoticed. I appreciate you.

To my children, whom I love with all my heart. Because of you all, all I wanted to do is something, anything with my life so that you can see with God all things are possible. You all are the reason I chose to live when I wanted to die.

To my grandmother in heaven, thank you for loving me and nurturing me during your brief time here on earth. The bond we had cannot be described in words. Just know that your "Jack" is living the way you desired. Even though I did not finish beauty school as you dreamed for me, I still think you would be proud of the path I took.

Contents

Dedication iii

Acknowledgment iv

Foreword vi

Preface 1

Chapter One: The Beginning 2

Chapter Two: The Big Move 12

Chapter Three: The Loss 21

Chapter Four: Lost 25

Chapter Five: That Winning Spirit 31

Chapter Six: The Descent 40

Chapter Seven: Picking Up the Pieces 44

Chapter Eight: Yes, I Can 49

Chapter Nine: The First Lady 53

Chapter Ten: A New Me 57

Epilogue/Conclusion 59

About The Author 60

Foreword

When I met Ronica, I did not know that God was allowing me to be a part of a remarkable journey of watching the love of my life grow into a phenomenal woman, wife, and friend. The love she gives friends and family is unconditional and long-suffering. I thank God for allowing me to be an eyewitness to the anointing that He has draped over this incredible lady.

Trauma II Triumph takes us through the journey of a little girl searching for identity, acceptance, and love. Ronica creatively articulates every detail of her life without deviating from the truth. This book will not only help you understand who Ronica is, but it will challenge you to peel back the layers of your own trauma.

Though this book is a memoir of Ronica's life, it is also the story of so many men and women who were exposed to physical and sexual abuse at a young age. I pray that Trauma II Triumph will encourage those who have experienced this type of trauma to seek professional help. I hope it sends the message that no matter where you are in your life, "You are fearfully and wonderfully made;' Psalms 139:14.

I am honored and Proud to be the Pastor, Husband, and Best Friend of this courageous and beautiful author. To whoever reads this book, I just want you to know that "You Matter."

Pastor Adrian

Preface

My dream for my memoir is for people to see a piece of themselves in my story. Trauma unfortunately happens to a lot of us, and we are taught as people not to speak on things to protect the images of others. However, people suffer in silence, not feeling like they have a voice or that they even matter.

I do not wish to tarnish or destroy the legacies of anyone or anyone's likeness mentioned in my memoir. With teenage parents, I am sure, in retrospect, there are some things that my birth mother and father wish they could have done differently.

Some parts of this story happened over thirty years ago, and since then, my father and I have worked and continue working on building a healthy relationship. I have done work on my healing in therapy for many years, spiritual healing, and spiritual guidance, and taking accountability for my actions and flaws. I would never intentionally demonize anyone, but this is MY experience.

Chapter One: The Beginning

One sunny day in August 1978, a six-pound baby girl was born to teenage parents. When life is supposed to be filled with love, happiness, acceptance, and belonging, this baby girl has a long, difficult road ahead of her. Unaware of the challenges life would bring, this baby's journey was about to begin. Thankfully, I hold to this scripture, "Before I formed you in the womb, I knew you. Before you were born, I set you apart; I appointed you as a prophet to the nations. Jeremiah 1:5."

My mother was sixteen years old in the eleventh grade with a boyfriend who was fifteen years old. Not being properly supervised, the inevitable would happen, and my mother would get pregnant. She hides this pregnancy as long as possible, but eventually, it comes out. So that my mother may finish high school many family members stepped up to babysit. This caused me to be passed from home to home and family member to family member. Experiencing no real connections, rejection was embedded in who I was from the beginning.

My father decided to take a different path. At the age of seventeen, he decided to join the United States Army. Vowing to return and get his family, he set off on a new career journey. As promised, he returned and married my mother when they came of age, and another child was born into that union. I got a little sister. Thank goodness, I would need her throughout my life's journey.

Problems arise when two young people try to play house too early. Not shocking, the marriage did not work, and my mother had to move in with her mother. My grandmother vowed to help raise us two girls. My grandmother and I developed a special relationship. It has been speculated that my grandmother was trying to make amends for neglecting to raise her own child, my mother, who incidentally was passed around from house to house as well, a generational curse; maybe or maybe not.

During my formable years, my maternal grandmother was a constant in my life, making sure I had everything I needed, and the bond developed was just unbreakable. I found safety, comfort, and love. I just felt special with her. She nicknamed me Jack. I remember people asking if my name was Jacqueline. I would say no, and I would get that puzzled look. Then, my grandmother would explain that I looked like my paternal grandfather, whose name was Jack.

She told me he showed up at her home one day looking for the baby his teenage son had fathered. He wanted to help out. She told me she said to herself who is this white man at my door? He was African American but could pass for another race. She always called him white. But she stated his eyes looked familiar; she saw my eyes when she saw him, she began to call me Jack, and it just caught on with the rest of the family.

When I entered second grade, my mother decided to marry another gentleman we will refer to as the devil, also husband number two. This man was physically abusive to my mother well before she decided to marry him, but she decided to proceed anyway. My father had moved on, and I suspect she wanted to as well.

The devil wanted to move to Dallas, Texas, to pursue a break-dancing career, and that is when I started experiencing the devil as an evil stepfather. For some reason, the devil hated me. He was just mean-spirited when it came to me, but he liked my sister.

This man beat me for some of the dumbest reasons, almost like he set situations up to have a reason to beat me. I recall a situation where I did not want to eat something on my plate. He yelled and screamed as I sat at the table and cried my eyes out. Irritated, he snatched me up from the table and began to beat me.

A cousin who lived with us at the time intervened, and he jumped on her too. Instead of my mother bringing peace or intervening, she kicked my cousin out of the apartment who had moved to Dallas to be with her.

Another situation that happened, true to the little girl I was, I talked a little too much in class. Go figure, right? I found myself getting paddled by the principal but was too afraid to tell my mother or stepfather for fear of getting disciplined at home as well. On top of the paddling I received at school, I also had to write those dreaded sentences. "I will not talk in Mrs. Odell's second-grade class." I will never forget that.

Three hundred times for a second grader is excessive, but hey, apparently, it did not stop me from talking. My stepfather caught me in my room writing my sentences, and OMG, he snatched my papers and tore them up. I was almost finished, and my eyes saw red. I wanted to hurt him badly, but I was too small to do so. He then gave me new paper and made me write all three hundred sentences over again, one sentence at a time. I had written all of my I's, then my will's, and so forth until almost done. He was so hateful. A child should not experience hate to this magnitude.

In the third grade, we moved to a new community. I started to attend Dan D. Rogers Elementary School. Since we lived close to the school, I found myself having to walk to school alone, which was very new to me. At my grandmother's house a bus picked me up right out in front of our apartment.

I will never forget Patrick, a bully at school. He lived in our community, and I am not sure what grade he was in. He zeroed in on me immediately. I guess I was an easy target. I was not a fighter, just a sensitive little girl. Walking home was one of the most terrifying situations ever. Patrick beat me up every single day. I finally got enough courage to ask my mother and the devil for help.

As fate would have it, Patrick's father and my stepfather worked together. So, I thought relief was coming when we told his parents, things would get better. We went to Patrick's home to talk with his parents about the issue. Patrick denied ever touching me, and his parents believed he would never hit a girl. They flat-out said I was lying to get attention.

That next day was brutal. I was so afraid to go to school. After school, Patrick turned up the heat, and I literally thought he was going to kill me. He beat me in my head numerous times. I just gave up trying to fight back and took it. I laid my life down, and I remember telling God this is it. I do not even want to live anymore if I have to go through that every day.

I survived the attack and decided to do things a little differently. Either I would stay after school late until I thought all the walkers would be home, or as soon as the bell rang, I would run as fast as I could to make it home safely. He caught me a few times. This was a very horrible season for me. I did not want to live or go to school because of the abuse I was experiencing at home and at school.

A time would come when the devil beat my mother really badly, and she decided to leave him, finally. He threw a knife at her at the breakfast table that flew right above my sister's head, and it lodged in the wall. Remember that cousin that my mother kicked out, yes, we had to move into her apartment.

Some anxiety about my life was relieved because at least I was safe at home now, and I had to change schools again. There were some really cool kids in her complex, and my sister and I were able to make friends and go outside and play like normal kids.

This peace was short-lived. My sister's friend drowned in the swimming pool after she was pushed into the pool by another kid while she was skating around the complex. Unable to get out of the pool on her own, she was floating by the time I found her. I was just taking a walk when I found her. I ran to tell her mom because I could not swim.

The scream her mom let out pierced my soul. I watched her mom jump from the second-story balcony while simultaneously pulling out her hair. It was devastating. Her mom pulled her out of the pool and began CPR. I remember her throwing up spaghetti, and water was escaping from her lungs. The ambulance took her away, and she sadly passed away. Sadness followed us like a cloud; we played with her every day, and now she was just gone.

I went into the house, and I will never forget my cousin was listening to Don't Disturb This Groove by The System. Every time I hear this song, even now, it takes my heart and mind back to that day. That was not the end, though. The little boy who pushed her into the pool name was Sam. He reminded me of the little boy from the movie Problem Child. Our friends in the complex were so upset that he was responsible for this accident.

We begged Sam's mom to let him come outside, promising her that we were not mad at him but wanted to play. As soon as his mom closed her door, we jumped on Sam, paying him back for killing our friend and for pushing my little sister in the pool a few weeks earlier with her skates on. Thank God there were many people in the pool that day, and my sister was spared. Sam needed to learn a lesson that we did not trust his mom to teach him.

Things soon became unbearable again while in Texas. The devil started to come back around, and I did the only thing I knew to do. I figured out how to make a long-distance phone call and called my grandmother while home alone. I told her I could not take it anymore and I wanted to come home.

In true Betty Jean fashion, not long after, my grandmother showed up with her boyfriend Frank and my Uncle Andrew in a U-Haul. She told my mother, "I came to get the girls; you can go if you want, but I'm taking the girls." After admitting she could not make it on her own, her things were loaded into the U-Haul as well. The ride home was so satisfying, knowing I was going back to safety and love.

Betty Jean, my grandmother, was one of the best people I

have ever known, but she was not perfect. I remember going to Circle K with a note for my grandmother's six-pack of Miller Light and her cigarettes. More Menthols in a green pack, not the red, my note said. Back then, they let me buy it.

My grandmother also had the biggest heart, which led to people always living with us who were down on their luck. Which unexpectedly led to people having access to us. I remember an instance when the cashier at Circle K needed somewhere to live. His name was Bobby, and he moved right in.

In exchange for her hospitality, he promised to take us places, just us kids. I thought it was weird, but we saw Bobby all of the time at the Circle K, and he seemed friendly. He offered to take us fishing, I did not really want to go, not an outdoors type of girl, but I wanted to be nice.

We packed up the car and headed to the lake; myself, my little sister, and Bobby. While unpacking the trunk to go to the dock, I turned around, and Bobby kissed me in the mouth. I was paralyzed with fear. I got back in the car, ready to go home. When I got home, I told my grandmother, and she immediately threw Bobby right out.

That was the beginning, though. It seems like predators know which kids to prey on. Not long after that, my grandmother had a guy friend over for dinner, and my sister and I were sitting on the floor watching our shows. My grandmother was in the kitchen, and her friend was sitting at the table behind us. He kept making grunting noises as if he was trying to get my attention. I turned around, and he was pointing at his private area and sticking out his tongue. I did not say anything at the time, but I did tell my grandmother, and she cursed him out, and I never saw him again.

I know my grandmother would not ever intentionally put us in harm's way, but I settled in my mind that all men were dirty perverts. Not trusting anyone, my grandmother decided never to marry until "her girls were grown" so that she could ensure our safety.

Because of the unfortunate things that happened, I began to hate myself. I hated my name, my face, my hair, just everything. I would look at my sister and say why are these men not looking at her. I always thought she was prettier, so why me?

There was a girl at school who was beautiful. Her mom owned a store where she had the best clothes, and she had naturally curly hair and was so popular. People talked about her hair all the time. I envied her. Not liking myself, I had a clever idea for a child that I thought would make me feel better.

I had long hair; it was coarse but long. I thought if I could get a Jerry Curl, my hair would be like hers. Remember, I am a child, but my grandmother said yes, I knew she would. I did not tell her the reason; I just said I wanted a curl, so she got my sister and me

Jerry Curls. I did not get the results that I dreamed of. My hair fell out in certain spots; the kids laughed because of the chemical smell, and it was just a disaster. I hated myself even more. My once long course hair was now struggling to survive; my sister's hair fell out completely, and my mother and my grandmother had a falling out.

My mother felt my grandmother did not respect her wishes when it came to our hair, and the results were irreversible. My self-esteem was non-existent. I felt ugly, dark-skinned, nappy-headed, bad-skinned, and I was sad all of the time. The men that violated me, I could see their faces all of the time, and I felt cursed, looking for some light, hope, peace, something I could hold on to.

Chapter Two: The Big Move

My little sister had a cat named Fluffy. The cat was a gag gift to my cousin at her wedding. They were going to get rid of it, but my sister begged for it, and my grandmother said yes. Unfortunately, the kitty got fleas, and my sister and I got impetigo (puss-filled sores) so painful and gross.

One of the very few times my father visited us after the divorce, we just happened to be during that time. I could tell he was not pleased, and he took us to the military base to get medical attention. Those people pulled out those needles, and my sister got up and ran. They had to catch us. We got those shots, but not without a fight. Little did we know this would set up a series of events the whole family would regret.

My father wrote my mother a letter while stationed in Seoul, Korea, with his new wife. He asked for physical custody so that he could contribute to his responsibility of raising his girls. Truly, he was not pleased with that visit, figuring we were not being taken care of properly.

He told my mother she could go to school or pursue dreams that she was unable to do as a "single mom." My grandmother said NO very adamantly. With her hands tied, because technically we were not her children, she had to let us go. My mother seemed like she was trying to get us out of sight, out of mind, without thinking through the cons.

My grandmother asked us what we wanted to do. Honestly, my father seemed like the coolest dad ever. We saw him once every year or two, and when we did, he took us to Red Lobster, bowling and shopping. He bought us named-brand things that my grandmother would never buy, so in our minds, this was about to be a life full of shopping, nice things, and lavish living. Boy, were we wrong. He was in the military, and his house was like basic training.

My sister and I were so excited when we saw our new house on base. We had our own rooms for the first time, decorated beautifully in our favorite colors. We thought we had the greatest living conditions, aesthetically at least.

The first thing that happened was we were stripped of all of our clothes and shoes. According to our father, a person only needs five outfits: two Sunday dresses, one pair of tennis shoes, and a pair of dress shoes. Remember our Jerry Curls? Yes, it became a problem again. Our stepmother stated we would not ruin her sofa, so she took us to a Caucasian stylist who did not specialize in African American hair, and her solution was to cut our hair off. Now we look like boys, having to wear the same clothes, and starting a new school is stressful for children.

Soon, I did not feel welcomed in that home. My stepmother had this air like she did not want us there. It makes me wonder if she was in agreement with this custody arrangement or if she just went along with it to please my father. My stepmother would be upset if we went in the refrigerator without asking, something we were not used to at our grandmother's house. We had freedom to the food in the house, never having to ask for anything.

My sister and I got home from school one day and decided we would make some break and bake cookies. My stepmother was so upset when she got home that she asked us why we went in the refrigerator. Of course, we said we wanted a snack. She told us to eat the snack she laid out for us and to never go in her refrigerator without asking.

As punishment, we were made to eat cookies for breakfast, lunch, and dinner for a week. Most kids would love that, right? Well, not if you are sitting at a table where the parents are eating chicken, steak, and shrimp while teasing about how good their meal was while you have a plate of cookies and a glass of milk in front of you. It was torcher by day three, I was so hungry for real food.

Every morning before school, we had to deep clean our rooms. The rooms that we were so excited about became beautiful prisons. When we got home from school, we would have to face post-it notes on areas that were not clean to my father's standards.

One lick for this, two licks for that, and we would get all of our licks on Saturday mornings. My father had purchased some straps from Auto Zone to administer these "licks." Every Saturday of course, I would have plenty of "licks," I could never do right. Being forced to operate as a soldier was above what my mind could fathom.

We also had a corner lot that was full of trees. Trees equal leaves, and we had to rake every Saturday morning. We were not used to this type of labor, and we got there in October just in time for all the leaves to fall. My grandmother lived in an apartment. We had never seen acres of land and definitely not to work on. We absolutely hated working outside in the cold on weekends, especially after we got our licks.

Spirits crushed, we just wanted to go back home. This was my father's first time being a full-time dad, and maybe he did what he thought was best. People always think they can whip "spoiled" children into shape.

My grades suffered terribly. I had all F's and a D. We begged to call our grandmother sometimes. I needed to hear her voice but was told long-distance calls cost too much. That was my first bout with depression as a child. I knew we made the biggest mistake ever and I did not know how to make it right.

The arguments between my stepmother and my father started to be more intense and more frequent. My father was sleeping in the study. Things were bad. Then came the fallout, from my perspective and memory.

One night, my father told me he had physical training the following morning. He stated it would be cold when he returned, so he would get in bed with me since I had a double bed, and my sister had a single. I immediately felt uncomfortable, so I suggested my sister sleep with me, and he took her bed. My sister and I slept together all the time back home. He declined and insisted it be me. Now, remember, at this time, we had only been there for two months; it was full of drama, and my father had been missing for a great deal of our lives. The intimate bond between father and daughter was not there because he simply had been mostly absent up until this point.

I did not sleep well that night, and as planned, early morning, he climbed into bed with me. I remember being frozen with fear and physically frozen by his ice-cold body. From my recollection, he spooned me from behind and cupped his hand to pull me closer to him by my crotch area. His hand remained there as tears rolled down my face. I do not remember him leaving, but that evening, when my stepmother got home, I screamed at her, “Where were you this morning?” She stated she went to work early and kept asking me what was wrong. I finally answered, “He touched me!” She gathered her things, and she and I left the house in a hurry. She drove to her pastor’s house, and they prayed. I do not remember much from what happened at the pastor's house, just the praying.

We went back home, and as soon as we walked in the door, I could hear my father was furious. He asked my stepmother where we went, and the arguing started. I was so scared. I thought I could sneak to my room, but on my way up the stairs, he looked over the banister and yelled, "You told her that?"

Before I could respond, he threw a hot iron down the stairs. I ran for my life. In their house, we could not wear shoes. We left them at the door, so I did not even think to put shoes on when I left. There was snow on the ground at this time, and I ran barefoot down the highway.

I will never forget a pizza delivery driver who stopped and said he noticed I did not have a coat on or any shoes. He asked if I was in danger, and I could not even speak. He begged me to get in the car, and I did. He drove me to the hospital on base. When we got there, military police were everywhere. One came up to me with a blanket and said every MP on the base was looking for me.

I was told my father had been arrested, and I was released into the custody of my stepmother. A few days went by, and as a kid, I did not know what was going on legally. All I knew I needed my mother or my grandmother to show up.

One day, my stepmother came home from being out, and she told my sister and me to get in the car. We did not talk in the car, and I remember it was just a long ride. We pulled up to the back of this building, and a lady came out. My stepmother told us to get out of the car. She said this lady will take care of you guys and she drove off. It was Social Services; we had been delivered to the foster care system.

We were so afraid; I had never needed my grandmother so much in my life. They were looking for a home to place us in, but it was difficult because they did not want to split us up. I needed my sister she was the only sense of familiarity I knew at that moment.

At the time, we did not know that my stepmother told Social Services that no one in the family wanted us, and that is why they had us in the first place, which was not true. I do not know if she was told that in order to agree to the custody arrangement, but it was not true. My grandmother did not want us to leave her home, and she expressed that explicitly before we left. Mind you, all of this happened between October and December.

The foster home was not bad. The people were really nice. It was a couple who had a few children of their own and a huge dog. Now, anyone who knows me knows I am terrified of dogs. Years before, I was chased down by a dog who had jumped a fence, caught me on the steps, and bit me. From that moment on, I never trusted a dog.

While these people were nice to us, I was afraid to move

freely in their home because I was scared of the dog, so I was isolated a lot in our room. We again enrolled in another school, having to try to adjust all over again. We were teased we did not have proper clothes because the foster mother was waiting on Social Services to send a check for our necessities.

I felt so alone and confused. Not understanding why, I could not simply just go home. I want to reiterate we were not abused or mistreated in this foster home. The family was as great as they could have been to us.

Legal proceedings begin a few months later. The end goal was to save my father's military career, in my opinion. My mother, favorite aunt, and paternal grandmother showed up for court. I thought we were in a legal proceeding about what happened that night, but the legal proceedings were actually about whether my mother had the means to get custody of her children back. They talked about my mother's income, her housing situation, her support system, and why she gave her children away.

I cannot recall how long all of this took, but with having to travel from Arkansas to Missouri for court and supervised visits, my mother lost her job and apartment and had to move back home with my grandmother, and the entire family was nearly bankrupted paying for legal fees to get us back home to Arkansas.

The day we found out we were going home was the best day

of my life at that point. I remember walking into my grandmother's house and feeling relief that all the weight fell off me. I hugged my grandmother so tight I did not want to let go. I did not know the difficulty that would lie ahead for me. Social Workers had to come to inspect our living conditions for a while, but it was not a problem because my grandmother always made sure we had what we needed. This was more of an inconvenience.

As a condition of release back to our family, there was an agreement for me to see a therapist. Nothing wrong with therapy, but I felt like they were trying to force me into saying I dreamed this or I misunderstood, and by the time I left therapy, I was more confused. I did not know what was real or not real anymore. I am an advocate for therapy. I see one until this day, but I feel like an agenda had been set to make me look like a lying, troubled child. I eventually just stopped talking. What I said did not matter anyway.

From that point on, I decided to stay silent on any wrongs I felt were against me. I felt no one believed me; I did not matter, and I was so confused I just figured I would hold everything inside. My voice had been stolen from me, and there was no way to get it back. I often cried for no reason, just depressed and wondering why I was alive. Did I have a purpose? If so, my purpose was in a dark cave, and I did not have the courage to enter that dark cave to get it.

Chapter Three:
The Loss

As fate would have it, my grandmother suddenly fell ill. I was fifteen years old then, and my grandmother always wanted me to rub her arms because they hurt so badly. I asked her all the time to go to the doctor, but she responded, "I don't need no doctor. It's just cancer eating me up." I would beg her not to say that, thinking she was older, maybe guessing or joking as she usually did with me.

Well, on a Thursday in late November 1993, we got a call from my grandmother's guy friend. We had been spending the night at a cousin's house. He told us he rushed her to the hospital because she was short of breath. In my mind, that was nothing serious. We rushed up there and laughed, talked, ate her dinners, laid in the bed with her, and just waited for test results so she could come home.

We went to the hospital every day. On Sunday, November 21, 1993, I called the hospital before going to church. I wanted to speak with my grandmother to tell her we would be there as soon as we got out of church. A nurse answered and told me she was resting.

Right before church started, my grandmother's guy friend busted in the front door of the church. When I saw his face, my heart dropped, he yelled: "She's gone!" I almost fainted. We were not expecting this. We knew she was coming home. We made it to the hospital, and looking at her lifeless body was too much to bear. I crumbled in disbelief. I had just spoken with her the night before and ate her hospital Jello and cookies at dinner time.

The doctor entered the room and informed us she had passed away of lung cancer that had spread to her breasts, stomach, and arms. The cancer had covered one lung and was throughout the other. He told us to break it down. Her entire upper body was affected by cancer.

We had questions like did she know when she passed? He explained to us that he gave her test results early that morning while she was alone, and she was devastated. The doctor says that she told him she would not be a burden to her girls and she did not want to live like that. He left the room, and she coded. I really wish he would have told her in our presence so we could have reassured her that she would be no burden at all, and we needed her. However, she made her decision and passed the way she wanted.

While grieving, my mother and her husband left the hospital and went straight to my grandmother's apartment and cleared it out completely. I was shocked I did not have time to process the death and certainly not for our home to be cleared out the same day.

My mother gave away everything my grandmother cherished. I remember my grandmother bought this white dining room table with white chairs, just beautiful. She said this is for the

President. If he is not here, do not sit at my table. My mother just gave it away. I was upset because I was there when my grandmother got that dining set, and she was proud of it. Everything on that U Haul my mother gave away to people whom either my grandmother did not know or care for.

I knew my grandmother's final wishes, we talked about it often. She used to joke and say when she goes, I would jump in the casket with her because we were so close, and I told her yes, I would. No one else gave a damn about me. She told me to take all of her jewelry when she passed. She wanted me to have it. She also told me what funeral home she wanted for her funeral. Before I could voice my grandmother's wishes, my mother had given away just about everything. I found one ring, and I stole it. That was all I had of my grandmothers. It was also the week of Thanksgiving, which is a blur to this day. We were preparing for my grandmother's funeral and Thanksgiving that week, and I was in a daze.

On Saturday, November 27, 1993, that day came—to say our final goodbye. I was angry and sad. I glanced at my grandmother in that casket and was infuriated. I know she would not have approved of her hair or makeup. They had this horrible stiff hairstyle that she would not wear in life and awful red lipstick. I told them I was not viewing her like that.

One thing I remember is one of my grandmother's co-workers stood up for acknowledgments. She said who is Jack? The nickname my grandmother gave me when I was a baby. I turned around, and she said Jack, your grandmother loved you. She talked about you every day at work. That gave me some comfort in the middle of this storm.

Then my two cousins, who begged my mother to be on the program, got up and sang It is So Hard to Say Goodbye to Yesterday originally by Boyz II Men. I have two words for that mess: AW FUL. People stopped crying and were stunned. My great-grandmother sitting at the front of the chapel in her wheelchair, sad because she had lost her firstborn, said, "Betty would have got up if she heard that shit." That was kind of funny looking back.

Chapter Four:
Lost

With my grandmother gone now, we were with my mother full-time. Grieving, new school, new neighborhood, I was lost. My mother had married into a new family, husband number three. The good thing is his family provided me with cousins my age, his parents had Sunday dinners with the entire family, and they lived close to us. I needed people at that time.

Most importantly, hanging out with my new cousins, we were made to go to church and go to choir rehearsal to sing in the choir on Sundays. I was afraid at first, I got baptized at ten years old, but this was different. I was good at something, and when I sang, it was therapeutic, like God was cleansing my soul. Even though we were being made to do this, I needed it. I found gospel music to become my lifeline, and I started to experience God in an unexplainable way.

The pastor made a real connection with me. I will never forget him. He let me sing. I wanted to do other ministry projects in the church, and he never told me no. I eventually ended up being the choir director. We were the family in the church with the money, so I did a lot of things at the church, funded by my stepfather. I needed that, though, because it took my mind off of my troubles.

I had one song that I led, and a lot of times, as the service would move along and it would be time for my pastor to preach, he would ask me to sing my song. I was like, wow, there are great soloists in this choir. Why would he want me to sing this song? I'm not even that good. I will never know. I loved him, though. I thought he was genuine and cared about me. I found refuge in that church, and I needed that at the time.

This story ended when my mother accepted her call to preach the Gospel. Women preachers were so taboo back then in a traditional Baptist church, and he told her you can preach all you want, but not in my pulpit. We left the church so that my mother could explore her calling—into ministry.

We joined a megachurch for about a year, and none of us was truly fulfilled. I wanted to do something in ministry like I always had, but in a megachurch, there is some rank to gain before you operate in ministry. My mother worked with a lady who invited us to her church, Church of God in Christ. I did not know what that meant at the time. I had not been exposed to doctrines; I just thought churches had different names.

She came over before church to give us a briefing, different from anything we ever felt or saw, she said. Guess what? It was. On the first visit, the pastor called me up and said those girls who have been messing with you, from this day forward, they will not be able to come near you. The holy spirit has a hedge of protection around you. I did not know this man that day, but he became my next pastor. I felt the holy spirit for the first time. I was interested in the Word, and he broke it down so I could understand. Watching him operate in his prophetic gift was amazing, and I got addicted to being in worship. As a teen, I did not miss church or bible study.

So, about the girls bullying me. From the time I moved with my mother full time, I entered a new school district. A group of girls declared war on me from the beginning. In seventh grade, I was called ugly, bald-headed, and threats of violence every day. I really went from grieving to being bullied again. I had one friend named Michelle. She had a baby in the seventh grade, so they ostracized her, too. All we had was each other. No one else liked us.

In eighth grade, one of the bullies told me I was pretty, but I was still ugly to her. Ninth grade was better because the high school was a bigger school, and I did not see them as often, but when I did, it was hell. They got other kids to join in throwing things at me on the bus. I had a couple of friends, but they were not with me all of the time, especially not on the bus. They lived in different neighborhoods.

Every grade got more intense. By eleventh grade, I was exhausted. I wanted to drop out of school, die, or kill them. One day on the bus they threw a bottle at me, and I had enough. Today was the day to fight back. They jumped me, but I gave all I had. Did I win? No, but I showed them I was tired of their shit.

That evening I had to work at the neighborhood grocery store, a job I started when I was sixteen. I needed this job to take care of my sister and me. We did not feel like my mother was providing our needs or wants, so I got a job. Well, one of the young ladies came to my job with a knife. I called my stepfather, and he came. She was already gone, but my stepfather was livid. He went to their house and spoke with her mother, shotgun in hand. He told her if she wanted her daughter, she better instruct her to leave his daughter alone, or she would find herself without one.

After that, the family took turns waiting at my bus stop, coming by my job, and just making sure I was safe. I still do not understand why bullies do what they do, but the experiences are traumatic, and that trauma lasts a lifetime.

Other than the bullying, I was the typical teenager, boy crazy and all. I had a lot of anger built up, and I rebelled. I despised my stepfather to some extent, and I despised my mother in some areas, too. They were so strict I could not do anything. I have never attended a dance, homecoming, football, or basketball game, nothing. In my mind was a prisoner again.

I would say I am walking to the park and my stepfather would follow me in his car and then ride by the park constantly until

I went home. It came to a point I just did not leave the house. But I was still searching for something. With the absence of a father's love, boys were the next best thing.

The first boy I latched on to name was Junior. I believe that I liked him way more than he liked me, and every week, there was another girl confronting me at school. He took every opportunity to humiliate me. Finally, I said no more and left him alone when he got a classmate pregnant. Then, I would do the unthinkable.

We had a substitute teacher, not in my classroom, just on the same floor. All the girls would whisper in the hallway about how fine he was, and yes, he was that fine. My friend and I were standing at our lockers, and I said I was going to give him my number. She dared me. I knew he was an adult, but I told you all I was searching for love. He actually showed interest, and that was all it took for me. In my mind, everyone wants him, but he wants me. I needed to feel wanted.

Since I could not go anywhere outside of school, I started skipping school to be with him. I had my first sexual encounter with him and found things out about my body that I simply did not know. Sex was not discussed in my home at all. We had to figure it out. I had no clue what an orgasm was. I remember being embarrassed when it happened the first time. He took his time with me, though, and I cared about him a lot. From then on, he was like an addiction to me.

Good things do not last long. Well, what I thought was a good thing. Unfortunately, my uncle's girlfriend knew his wife. I had lied and told my mother he was only nineteen. I knew he was older, but I could not tell her that. And he had a wife! I was so angry with him, but he told me they were separated, and I believed him. Remember, I started dating him when I was fifteen. He could have told me anything. In my mind, I needed him.

Already in self-destruct mode, I did not care about his marital situation. I knew it was wrong, but he made me feel so right. At the time, I needed to feel good and distracted, and this situation made me feel good from being bullied and from grieving. He chose me, he loved me, he picked me up from school in front of other kids, got my hair and nails done. At the time, I needed that attention.

This love affair lasted ninth, tenth, and eleventh grade and most of my senior year. I got tired of the lies and feeling bad because I knew this was wrong (the Holy Spirit). I told him I could not be with him anymore. I had to quit that addiction cold turkey. It was a horrible feeling of withdrawal, but a new ride was loading.

Chapter Five: That Winning Spirit

After this breakup, I was devastated. I had one semester left of my senior year. I dated another guy, but it was only causally, of course, he was older. School-aged guys just did not interest me. Unbeknownst to me, he was dating a girl the next street over. She found out about me and was playing on my phone, calling the house at all times of the night.

It was a problem because my mother and her husband had just had a baby girl who was born with a hole in her stomach. Just coming home from surgery, it was imperative our house be quiet so the baby could rest. I explained to this crazy girl that she could have this guy; it was not that serious, and he pursued me. She kept calling, so I pleaded to her that my baby sister was sick and please stop calling, but she told me to "fuck myself and my sister." I unplugged the phone.

The next day, this girl showed up at my bus stop and I was enraged about the comment she made about my sister. She wanted to fight, and I was about to give her exactly just what she wanted. Her child's father just happened to be riding by, stopped this altercation, and begged her to go home. As she was leaving, she yelled, "He's mine bitch," and I told her well I would rather have your child's father instead. Why did I do that? Her child's father became my boyfriend shortly after that. He had a girlfriend, but after we started dating, he broke up with her. He took me to my senior prom, and we were just two broken people trying to be normal.

Shortly after, I became pregnant while a senior in high school. I was so scared. I did not know what to do. I told him, he had already had one child and did not want another, and I could not let my mother find out. My stepfather always said he was so strict because he was not raising any other kids. My boyfriend's guardian breached my trust and told my mother, and she was livid.

I was so sick from this pregnancy that I could not even hear her fussing because I had a constant headache and constant nausea. My mother gave me an ultimatum: get an abortion or get out. I did not have anywhere to go. My grandmother was gone, and we did not have a family like that. I felt I did not have a choice. So, they came up with the money, and I got an abortion as a senior in high school. I hated everyone for forcing me to do that and for telling me it was for my own good.

A few months passed, and it was time for my senior activities: senior breakfast, prom, and graduation. My mother was still upset with me for getting pregnant, so we did not talk a lot, plus she had her own new baby. I got to attend my senior activities, but that is it.

My father paid for my prom attire, and I was able to attend prom, but my mother said to come home right afterward. Yeah right. My boyfriend and I had already booked a room at the hotel, and I had no intentions of going home on prom night. Well, my mother called someone. I do not even remember how I got the message, but she told me not to come home at all. I got kicked out on prom night. So, I partied hard.

After partying hard, I called my big cousin. I did not have a lot of options for places to go. With nowhere else to go and nothing but a prom dress on, that was rented, I found myself sleeping on my cousin's couch.

A few weeks later, I begged to come home. I missed my sister, and that couch was hard. Graduation day was approaching, and I could not wait. I made up my mind I was leaving home after graduation. The big day came, and my family attended. My father and his wife came into town, and this was supposed to be a joyous occasion.

My mother despised my stepmother and refused to attend dinner with us. We went to Red Lobster with my father's side of the family, and I believe my mother was still angry with me for getting pregnant. When I got home, I begged to go to a graduation party, I was eighteen years old and graduated, but my mother refused. That made me want to leave even more.

I had a job, so I started buying home goods after graduation, not knowing how or when I was leaving, and I wanted to be prepared. My mother and I were not seeing eye to eye on my choices, and I wanted to do what I wanted to do.

Earlier in my senior year, I took the ASVAB to go to the military, but when my mother found out, she flipped out. She threw the recruiter who wanted to meet with her about my options out of our home. This was a way out for me, but it did not work. I always wonder how different my life would have been if I had gone to the military.

The only thing for me to do was to get out on my own. One month after graduation, my cousin had a friend who sublet an apartment for me. Of course, it was me and my boyfriend. The rent was $325, and my boyfriend and I were working, so we figured we could do this. So many things went wrong.

The first night we moved in, I had to work. My boyfriend dropped me off, and things should have been fine. They had too many people at work, so they sent me home. Remember no cell phones back then, so I waited until I thought he would be home, and called, and there was no answer. I called his childhood guardian and told him, and he agreed to pick me up and take me home.

I put my key in the lock, and the chain was on the door, so I was knocking and screaming. My boyfriend opened the door, and he was there with the chick he broke up with for me. She had a smirk like she got one over on me, and I lost my cool. Of course, he lied his way out of it. She needed closure, he said. Like a dummy, I let it go because people were looking down on me for “stealing” him in the first place.

Times got hard for us. I got laid off, and his hours got cut. We could not pay the bills like we thought, and arguments about finances became the norm. He came up with this great idea. The story I was told is his sister was getting divorced and needed help financially. She had a room we could rent, and it would help us and her.

Mind you I had only met this lady once or twice, so no personal relationship. I went along with it; we moved in, and we had a nice room. She had a beautiful home, but I felt confined to my room. I did not know her like that; he was always gone, and her husband never left. I was trapped now.

I found a little night job, and I would go to work at night and sleep during the day. Then I found out I was pregnant again. This time was different. I was grown and could make my own decisions. We were happy, I thought. I came home early from work one night, and he had a girl over at his sister’s house. I was so mad I keyed his car. He and the girl jumped in the car and sped away.

In the middle of the night, I walked to my mother's house and asked if I could come home. Her marriage had fallen apart by then, so we needed each other. I needed a place to live, and she needed a babysitter for my little sister. She gave me her car, and I went over to his sister's home, packed all of my belongings, and returned home to my mother in the middle of the night. I found out later the girl was his sister's husband's niece and everyone in the family knew about this relationship but me. I played the fool.

I was about six months pregnant with my daughter when we found out my mother's home was in foreclosure. The sheriff knocked on the door and said we had to be out by Tuesday. We had five days to leave. Now, I am pregnant and basically homeless. After putting our life in storage, we went to live with a relative.

It is hard to live with someone, especially when it feels like an inconvenience to them. It was on the other side of town, out of the way of the life we lived, my sister's school, my doctor's office, and so forth. My mother made the decision for us to move in with her in-laws. How embarrassing, but they welcomed us with open arms, did not want a dime, and my "step-grandmother" wanted to take care of me because I was pregnant. She made sure I ate healthy and was wonderful to me.

I carried a bit of shame and humiliation. I am alone, pregnant, homeless, and broke. However, I focused on my baby.

When I went into labor, I sat in the closet and muffled my screams all night. I did not want to worry anyone with my problems, already feeling like a burden.

When morning came, I got dressed as normal and told everyone I had an appointment. I caught a ride to the doctor's office. When they finally checked me, my baby's head was crowning. They told me I was in active labor. I already knew that, but I was young. The nurse from my doctor's office took me across the street to the hospital to prepare for labor.

I was so scared and alone. The anesthesiologist came in and explained the epidural procedure to me. Scared of needles, I told him no thanks. He laughed and said, "I'll see you later." I chose Demerol instead, and those labor pains hit me so hard and I told my nurse, "Go find that white man." He entered the room with the biggest smile on his face. He told me he knew he would see me again. "Just do it," I told him, and thank God it begins to work. I gave birth alone, then called the house and told them I had a baby girl.

My doctor left town without discharging me, a mistake on his part. However, I used that week in the hospital to relax, regroup, and think about my next steps. I had a baby girl now, and I had to think bigger than me.

Once discharged, I went home with a fire in my heart. I could not remain homeless. My step-grandmother helped with the baby. I had support at home. They would hold her while I showered and let me take naps and hold my baby when I got overwhelmed. Not wanting to be a burden, my crying baby would frustrate me at night. I would beg her not to cry, but my step-grandparents were so gracious. They would say, “We didn’t hear a thing,” but I know they did. I needed my own place; at six weeks post pregnancy, I got a retail job, and with every check, I would pay my $60 per week daycare fees, then put the rest in a money order to save up for my own place.

God came through for me. I got a brand-new apartment for $400 per month. I was not of age yet, but the manager, a sweet lady named Sunny, waived that for me. I was initially awarded $395 per month from the housing authority but when they inspected the apartment, they declared it was too much room for me and a baby. I declined their assistance and started my new journey alone.

No furniture or anything. I slept in this brand-new empty apartment with my baby, but it was mines, and no one could throw me out, and I did not feel like a burden. My baby could cry freely. It was a great feeling. I did something on my own.

When God shows up, so does the devil. My child’s father reached out. He wanted to be with his family, he said. I wanted a family desperately, too, so I let him move in. He worked hard and furnished the apartment, and things were fine for a while.

Shortly thereafter, I was pregnant again. This time, I was ashamed because I honestly did not want any more children but was not getting an abortion. At the same time, my pastor found out my child's father lived with me and told me if I wanted to continue operating in ministry, I had to get married. I was so addicted to God's presence that I gave him the ultimatum: get married or get out. We got married.

On our wedding day, I was all nervous. God had been speaking to me all morning. It was audible. I heard God's voice telling me this was not his plan for me. My pastor forgetting my wedding that day should have been a red flag, but they called him, and he came to the church. I was shaking all the way down the aisle because I knew this was a mistake, but I was in too deep. Plus, my baby deserved a father, and the baby no one knew about yet needed a father, too.

Chapter Six: The Descent

After giving birth to my son, I fell ill with the flu. I was partially coherent but in bed most of the time. My new husband told me he was going to meet a cousin. I did not care, but I should have. I do not remember when he came home. I was so pumped up with medication.

The next morning, I was watching the news, and two gentlemen had been robbed, murdered, and sat on fire in the trunk of their car, left in a remote field. I remember thinking how awful that was, but I did not know them personally. It was tragic. As time went on, I could tell a decline in my husband's spirit. He was smoking pot more frequently, he got fired from his job, and he was irritable all of the time.

I finally told him I could not go on like this, so he confided in me that he was present for a robbery. I was devastated. He brought to my remembrance the murders that had been all over television. He told me he was forced to participate in the robbery but left before the murders took place. My world came crashing down.

About six months later, detectives started to snoop around. I told him to get an attorney before making a statement. No one listens to me, though. The detectives "befriended" him, and he gave a full confession, thinking they would help him because he was a good person, right? A few days later, they arrested him for aggravated robbery. I almost fainted, thinking, what am I going to do? He was bonded out by his childhood guardian, but after more investigation, his charges were upgraded to two counts of Capital Murder.

This was the absolute worst time. It was all over the news, people were whispering, I was scared to death because they put our address in the newspaper. These guys had loved ones who could have retaliated, and I had my children to protect. To make matters worse, my landlord saw the article and evicted me because the address was listed publicly.

I had to move in with my mother, who did not make us feel comfortable. I was a burden again. I had to do something. I applied for an apartment thirty-five minutes away in a new community so that my children could be safe and would not have to face the whispers and people judging me. Two weeks later, I got a call on a Sunday that I could move in. That day, I took my children, and we slept in our new place on the floor until I could get my things out of storage.

Things were okay for a few months. I was working full-time and in beauty school part-time. I could tell that my husband became distant again and I knew something was wrong. He started getting pages in the middle of the night, and all of a sudden, he got switched to the night shift at the water plant.

One night, I got home from beauty school, and he was still awake when I got home. Tired from work and school, I was about to turn in. My husband said he needed to run to the store and asked if I needed anything. I told him no; he left the house and never came back. At first, I was worried because people wanted to kill him. I thought maybe they caught him slipping.

I called his childhood guardian and told him my husband was missing. He assured me that my husband was not missing, but he was not at liberty to tell me of his whereabouts, but he was safe. I knew at that moment it was someone else and I threw all of his belongings in the garbage and threw my wedding ring in the pond in front of our apartment. Now, I had to pick up the pieces of my life, left alone again with two toddlers. I moved from that apartment. It was so far away from everything, especially as a single mom now.

A month went by, and I went to work after Christmas break. My supervisor jokingly said he had a dream about me. I jokingly said, "I did not die, did I? and he said no. I said well, I know I am not pregnant; I do not have a man. We laughed about it, but the statement resonated in my heart and mind, and I could not shake it.

I took a pregnancy test, and I was pregnant again. I was so shocked I did not know what to do. I cried for days. I am about to be a pregnant divorcee. I fell into a deep depression. I had a four-year-old, a three-year-old, and pregnant again. The embarrassment was too much for me to bear. Some people criticized me, and in disbelief, I was pregnant again. There were a few people who stepped up to help me. The love was overwhelming. I believe they felt sorry about my situation, but whatever the motivation, God was looking out for me.

In the end, my husband took a plea in exchange for his testimony against the others and was sentenced to ten years in prison. He had already left me, but the fact that he went to prison was embarrassing in itself. I had two babies, pregnant with a third, my husband in prison, and in agonizing despair.

Chapter Seven: Picking Up the Pieces

Now I know exactly what I have: me. I immersed myself in ministry, God's Word, and vowing to change my life. In my new place, I was still battling depression. My children were so little and needed so much needed attention, but I had nothing to give. I cried so much the tears burned my face.

My four-year-old daughter would hold me while I cried. She had to grow up fast to take care of me and my son. People used to say she was so grown up, but she had to be. I did not know if I was coming or going. I tried to put on a face outside of my house, but when I got home, I crumbled. This went on my entire pregnancy.

When I got ready to give birth, I asked a friend to keep my kids, and I made her promise she would not tell anyone where I was. I wanted to give birth peacefully and alone so I could think. My nurse was concerned when I checked in all alone. She pressed me about family, but I told her I did not have anyone. She called my emergency contact, which was my sister and asked her to come. My sister lived about an hour away at the time, but she came to be with me. I was mad at my nurse, but I am glad she called my sister.

Now home with a new baby girl, I had a renewed mindset: my kids and that is it. I made the difficult decision to file for bankruptcy and divorce at the same time. I needed a fresh start. Later that year, my divorce was final, and my bankruptcy had been discharged. A fresh, clean slate for me to do something different.

I was lonely, though, and felt like I needed a companion, an adult to talk to. Remember that substitute from high school? I found him. I called and asked if we could be friends again. I did not want to date new people, with my kids being so little, but I was familiar with him. He told me he was not married anymore, and we had chemistry more than anyone else I had ever been with. He knew me from the time I was fifteen years old.

This time, it was different; I was a grown woman, and our relationship was more intense romantically than it was the first time. I went in initially wanting a friend with benefits, but we fell in love again. We started to plan a wedding, and I thought this was it. He was a deacon at his church now, and I was deep in my faith as well. Soon, this great sex would be sin-free, and I would not have the guilt of that anymore.

Then God started to speak to me, he told me this is not it. I went back and forth with God. I love him, God. He loves me. It is meant to be because we came full circle, back together again, and God said no. I begged God for a sign, and he gave it to me. Shortly after, we got into an argument about the kids one night. We were in the bathroom, and he slapped me and began to choke me. I could not believe this. He had never been violent towards me before, ever. I told God I hear you. A few days later, I invited him over and broke off our engagement. I was honest and told him that I loved him wholeheartedly and wanted nothing more than to be his wife, but God did not approve, and I was not about to disobey God again in that area.

I cried for months, but I knew I did the right thing. For the next few years, I gave all of me to Christ. Being a single mom was hard, but I can honestly say that God provided all of our needs. He sent people in my life who had kids just a little older than mine, and they would give me clothes, shoes, coats, and brand-new stuff.

A lady at my son's daycare took a liking to him, and I never had to buy him anything while she was a part of our lives. Every season, she gave my son everything he needed. She shopped way too much for her son, and she would give my son everything. Another lady at the daycare "Mrs. Margie" treated my kids like her grandkids. She had a wealthy son who wanted to be a blessing to kids because he did not have his own. She would take my kids' Christmas list, and he would buy everything on the list, no strings attached. When I trusted God, he came through. Through trial and error, I began to give every situation to God.

Time passed, and I had been dating a guy who came with a lot of drama. His baby mama would call me constantly, wanting to fight, and I was just too grown to be participating in that. It was like he always had a new woman with new drama. I was faithful to him, and I liked him. He was an executive and made plenty of money, he was generous. After he would get caught cheating or after a woman would call me, he would bait me back in with what I needed most: money. He knew I was a struggling single mom, and he could do what he wanted because I would take his money for my bills. After a while, I did not care anymore because I knew how to get his money.

Tired of being tired, I decided I was not being faithful to a person not being faithful to me. I was so depressed, feeling so unworthy, my self-esteem tanked, and I wanted to give up on life. I went to work one day just out of it. I was crying constantly, just feeling like I would never be worthy enough for someone to choose. My natural father did not choose me, my ex-husband did not choose me, and this fool was basically torturing me, and I was at my lowest point.

A co-worker/friend took me to the hospital, worried about me, and they admitted me into the psychiatric ward on suicide watch. No television, no people, nothing but myself in a room so that God could shake me. People look at this as a terrible thing, but I needed that week to be purged by the holy spirit. My spiritual leaders visited me to pray, and I appreciate them holding me up in the spirit during that time. Without God, that could have been it for me. I was fragile.

After I got out of the hospital and some time went on, I was strong enough to have a real conversation with God. I was so exhausted; I was tired of this relationship; women were calling me still, and this man was lying still. He actually got another girl pregnant and asked me for money so this girl could get an abortion and he could "be with me." I told him to kick rocks.

I had a long conversation with God that night. I told him, that the next man who asks for my number, I am going to give it to him. God has a sense of humor because that very next day, I met my current husband at the mall, and he asked for my number. I told God, I hear you.

Chapter Eight:
Yes, I Can

With this newfound friendship/romance, Adrian spoke life into me. He was so nice; he took the time to learn things about me. I could mention something l liked just in casual conversation, and he would surprise me with it. He gave me the attention that I needed and made me feel special.

We spent quality time together, and my kids were not an issue for him. He wrote me poems and love letters, and I honestly never had that before. There were times when he gave me his last dime. I had never been loved like this before. With the odds stacked against me, he broke down what I thought were barriers in my life. He asked me if I ever thought about attending college. With three kids, I did not think that that would be possible. I did not have proper childcare for that, and he told me about attending online. I did not know that was a thing, so I enrolled in college.

With my college funds, I fixed my credit and started to work out the barriers in my life, one by one, with his support. My kids loved Adrian, my family accepted him, and for the first time, things were perfect. All I needed was him. He came to my church and supported my role in ministry. He gave me confidence that I did not know I had.

With about a year of bliss, things would become complicated again. My new love was mobilized with his military unit and had to move away. He promised me that this was not the end, we could still be together long distance, and that he would come back for me. I was so used to people letting me down I was shaking my head yes, but my heart was saying yeah, right. I thought it was over. Mad at God, I asked why would you do this to me? Tease me with a hope of happiness. He told me to be still and know.

This man was true to his word. Adrian would visit often, and he would send for me, the first time I ever took a flight. He still encouraged me to pursue my dreams. We were physically apart but still emotionally connected. He sent for me in October of 2006, and on that trip, he proposed to me, and I said yes. We were far from rich, and the ring he gave was not the biggest, but I loved him and did not care. I was elated, and things were looking up for me. He chose me. Someone finally chose me.

During our engagement, so many people tried to hate our situation. They tried to plant seeds of doubt, asking me if I was stupid enough to believe he was not cheating on me. Did I actually believe he would come back and marry me when he had so many other options? People said if he did come to get me, he would move me out of town to isolate me from my family and beat me. I heard what they said, but I believed what God said. I knew this was it. I went forward with planning a wedding because I wanted nothing more than to be someone else. I desired to start over and live a life of happiness with a partner who chose ME.

As fate would have it, we got married in an intimate ceremony at The Old Mill in Arkansas. I was so happy. The day was almost perfect. I had asked my father to walk me down the aisle, on the day of my wedding, he called my mother to tell her to tell me he could not make it. That little girl inside was crushed, but I pushed through and married my sweetheart. We married on a Sunday afternoon, and the next day, I went to the DMV to change my name. My maiden name seemed like it was cursed in my mind, so I desperately needed a new name and a new start.

During this time, my ex-husband was released from prison and wanted to see his children. I did not have an issue with it; kids need their father. Drastic changes were in store for us, though. Due to my new husband's job, we would have to move to Virginia. It seemed like my ex got out one month, and then I moved two months later, but it was just a coincidence. I had to do what was best for me.

Things were not as rosy at first. I left a job I had been at for ten years, just knowing I would find something quickly, but that did not happen. In addition to that I found out we were expecting. I was so sick I could not work a job if I had one.

We had a beautiful baby girl, and I was unemployed for a couple of years, which put a strain on our marriage financially. The good thing about the situation is for the first time I got to bond with our baby. I always had to rush back to work to feed my family, but this time, I could spend time with her and witness all the milestones that I had missed with my other children.

I continued attending college online and graduated with an associate degree. My husband encouraged me to keep pushing, so I enrolled in a four-year university. Working on my degree and raising my baby girl, it came time for us to make a major purchase. We started to build our starter home.

I was so in awe of what God was doing in our lives that we drove an hour a few times a week to look at our hole in the ground and then every step of progress to our home. It was ours; we did this together. At the same time, my husband was a candidate to pastor a church and was installed as pastor shortly after. We bought a new home, and my husband began pastoring a church almost simultaneously.

Chapter Nine:
The First Lady

I had been in church since I was ten years old, but when you see the other side of ministry, you develop a new perspective. With my insecurities as a woman and not knowing how I would fit in at this church, I was very reserved at first, sitting all the way in the back. I had not been part of a Baptist church in years and honestly did not want to be a part of a Baptist church then.

I am far from a traditional religious church person. I do not like traditions without biblical explanations. I will ask why and expect a biblical answer. If not, I will not participate in doing things because people have always done them. However, I wanted to support my husband, but all I knew was what I saw other first ladies do growing up. Also, I had three school-aged children and a baby. I wanted to work in ministry but was limited at first because of my responsibilities at home.

As time went on, I started to become more involved. Maybe my personality was a bit much for some, but the women turned on me immediately. I believe there was one woman who influenced the others, but my experience was horrible. I was told I was unapproachable, I thought I was better than other people, and things I had not been told about myself before. I know I am an acquired taste because I am extremely introverted and not for everyone, but never been treated that badly as an adult. Meetings were contentious because I did not back down from a belief. I tried to make peace, but the other parties were not interested. I will stand for righteousness even if I have to stand alone. I stood alone a lot.

This caused me to go into depression again because I thought I was letting my husband down. In a meeting, “my enemy” yelled, “You are not a first lady. You are just his wife.” I slowly started walking towards her, not knowing what I would do, but the Jones in me almost surfaced. Thank God for the deacon who grabbed me. I could have lost the credibility of my ministry that night.

As the years passed, God started pruning that ministry. People started to die, move away, or move their memberships. Things were better and worse at the same time. My husband had fulfilled his assignment to that ministry, and God was preparing us to move on. I wholeheartedly believe that everything happens for a reason. The suffering I endured while serving in that ministry prepared me for the peaceful atmosphere at our next assignment.

I am so appreciative of the people we serve. We have a mutual respect for each other, worship is wonderful, and church business is easy, not one contentious meeting in the years we have served this branch of Zion. I tell them often that I appreciate the atmosphere they have created so that we may worship in spirit and in truth.

During this time, I obtained my bachelor's degree. This is why I know God is real. Shortly after moving into our home, I had to drop out of school. I had run out of financial aid and could not afford tuition out of pocket. I had five classes left. I tried everything but nothing was working out. I told God I was too close to let that degree slip away, and I needed a miracle.

About a year passed, and I kind of settled in my soul that the ship had passed. Then I got a phone call from my school. They had started a Reconnect Program and saw that I only needed five classes. The AVP of Academic Affairs asked why I dropped out, and I was honest. I told her I could not afford it. She told me they could sponsor me so that I could graduate. I finished my undergraduate degree while only having to pay for books.

I felt so accomplished I immediately signed up for the master's degree program. Every accomplishment made me hungry for more. A new journey began for me, and it was rough, but my husband was my biggest cheerleader. I got a D on a paper once and said to myself, "who am I kidding? I'm not smart enough to do this. I'm going to be grateful for the bachelor's degree I have." My husband told me not to let one setback make me a quitter. I dug in deep and accomplished my mission.

Being well-educated opened new opportunities for me. I landed a job doing something I love as a Human Resources Professional at a major higher education institution. It is easy for me because I love what I do. I needed to establish my own identity outside of my husband. My plan was to hide in the shadows of his accomplishments and be his Mrs. without my own worth or identity.

Everything I knew about myself I hated, but I loved everything about who I was with him. My husband taught me that I matter, that I am an individual, and I should have my own goals, dreams, and aspirations. Now, we complement each other, and I have enhanced the name he gave me.

Chapter Ten:
A New Me

With a new job, new ministry, and new confidence, I am walking with new authority. It is a blessing to finally come to an agreement with who God called me to be. I will be the first one to admit I am far from perfect, but I know myself now. I have an identity. I am honest with who I am, my strengths, and my weaknesses. I can say now that I have mental health challenges without being ashamed of the stigmas attached to them. I have major depressive disorder and social anxiety, and I own it.

My depression is real. I have encountered some really dark times, but I know there is light somewhere. I just got to press forward. I can have a span of greatness, and then a situation happens that could draw me back to a dark place. Now, I know nothing is final, and I have the tools to cope with my condition. Whether it be therapy, medication, or lifestyle changes, there are tools to cope with my condition that were unclear to me before.

There is no shame in who I am. I praise God through it all because I am fearfully and wonderfully made (Psalms 139:14). God did not make any mistakes while creating me. I can walk in victory knowing where I came from and where I am going. All the things that I have endured in life have made me the strong woman I am today.

I struggle with social anxiety, and I am extremely introverted. Sometimes, I have panic attacks when entering a room of strangers. Even when I am courageous enough to work a room by the end, I feel drained. Small talk, fake people, and superficial programs are draining, and it is ok. When I feel overwhelmed, I know that it will pass, and I am not desperate anymore to be accepted, invited, or dying to be in anyone's company. It really is ok. Sometimes, it hurts, and that is the human side of me, but life is just life, and people are just people.

I have ventured off into new things of which I am proud. I became an entrepreneur and proud owner of RLS Events & Entertainment; I took a risk, and I love it. I am a new author something I never even dreamed of, but I believe my story of trauma, endurance, and God's grace will bless others to keep moving.

I became a grandmother and loved it; those little eyes showed me unconditional love, and I remember how much my grandmother meant to me. I am striving to be the best Glam Ma ever because I was blessed with the best grandmother ever. I became a dog lover; well, I love my dog. I also dabble in content creation on social media platforms. I am just living life and being the best person I can be. There are so many wonderful things to life, and for you, my hope is that you rise above your trauma and trust God to do the impossible.

Epilogue/Conclusion

My prayer is that someone will be blessed by my story—that they believe that God can do anything but fail. I was bred in rejection and suffered a lot of traumas. I lost my lifeline (my grandmother) at the most critical time in my life. I searched for love in all the wrong places, begging for someone to choose me.

I was a single mom for a while, and I suffered through mental health challenges. With all of that, God still blesses me, uses me, and grants me victory in every situation. If he could do it for me, he can surely do it for you. Walk triumphantly in this life, I am, and you can. I believe in Psalms 138:8: The Lord will perfect that which concerneth me. I believe he will perfect what concerns you, too.

About The Author

Ronica Lynneshia Sledge, socially known as Ronnie Lynn, is a Human Resources Professional at the University of Virginia, certified by the Society of Human Resources Management (SHRM). She is also the Executive Pastor of the M.O.V.E! Church. Ronnie Lynn owns and operates RLS Events & Entertainment. She earned a Master's Degree in Public Administration from Capella University, a Bachelor's Degree in Interdisciplinary Studies from the University of Arkansas at Little Rock, and an Associates of Arts Degree from Pulaski Technical College. She also holds certification from Cornell University in Workplace Investigations. Ronnie Lynn and her husband have a blended family of ten children and twelve grandchildren. She currently resides in Culpeper, Virginia, a small town south of D.C. She loves to shop, spend time with family, and serve in ministry.

Made in the USA
Middletown, DE
01 May 2024

53737945R00040